Refinishing Pine Furniture

by Monte Burch

Is some of your furniture looking ragged? Do you have antiques in your attic that you would love to use, if only they looked a bit better?

If your answer to either question is yes, try furniture refinishing. It's not difficult, can be done during your spare time, the costs are not high, and the rewards are great, with deep satisfaction promised each time you look at or use your handiwork.

Where to begin? We suggest starting on a piece of furniture that is not a family heirloom, one with flat surfaces and few curlicues. You'll find pine easy to work with. It's easy to remove old paint from it, and a new finish goes onto its smooth surface in a most satisfying manner.

There are five steps involved in refinishing: stripping, surface preparation, staining, applying finish, and polishing that finish.

Ready for the first step?

Stripping

The hardest part of refinishing furniture is removing the old finish. Most antiques or primitives will have a substantial coating of finish, and in some cases several coats of paint. Several years ago I purchased a set of wooden church pews from a church that was being demolished. The old seats were painted an ugly green, and a scratch with a pocketknife revealed as many as a dozen coats of paint. After some labor with paint stripper I discovered the pews were solid walnut, with some very beautiful figured walnut.

Removing the finish from a wood surface can often be as easy or as hard as you want to make it. An old finish can often be removed from a flat surface by using a heavy duty belt sander, by running the wood through a planer, or even by using a torch to melt the old paint. All of these can cause more problems than they solve. The best solution is to use a chemical paint-and-finish remover or stripper.

The first rule is to stick to brand names when purchasing these products. Paint removers are like the old-time medicine show brews, some work and some don't.

Water-Washable Remover

For ease in working choose one of the water-washable removers. These can be hosed away, are less flammable, and don't raise the wood's grain as much as do some of the older types of remover. Make sure the stripper is a "semi-paste" type so it won't run off the surface too quickly.

Many people work too hard at this job. They brush on the paint remover, then immediately try to remove the paint. This results in too much time spent at the job and a waste of stripper. B.L. Bixeman, a manufacturer of a paint remover, was asked several years ago why his product wouldn't remove the paint from an old boat. He rolled up his sleeves, brushed a good coat of stripper on the boat, then took everyone out for coffee. When they came back

To apply paint remover, pour a small amount into a jar or can. Use a soft bristle brush to apply a full flowing coat. Wear old clothes, rubber gloves and either goggles or a face-shield.

most of the paint and stripper were lying in a puddle on the floor. *The point is to allow the stripper time to do the work for you.*

Safety Rules

But first a few safety rules and hints for working with paint strippers.

1. *Paint stripper is caustic.* Store it away from children and use it cautiously. Wear old clothes, rubber gloves, and goggles or a shop face shield.
2. *Make sure the area is well ventilated.* Removing paint is one job that is best done outside, especially if you can find a spot to hose off the remover. Watch out, though! Paint remover will kill grass.
3. *Have everything on hand for the job.* You'll need old newspapers to catch the remover drips, a hand scraper for removing stripper from around turnings and carvings, a can to hold the remover, and a soft bristle paint brush for applying the stripper to the surface.

Now you're ready. Let's start with doing a project outside because that is easier. If you need to work inside because of the weather, do the stripping work inside, then take the piece of furniture outside and hose it down as the last step.

Paint remover shouldn't be used in temperatures above 85° F. or directly in the sun. Heat has a tendency to bake the remover into the finish which makes it extremely hard to remove both the finish and the stripper.

One Surface

Work on one surface at a time. To prevent marks where you started and stopped, plan on completing any flat surface such as a table or desk top in one session. Don't attempt to do the entire project at one time, particularly if there are several layers of paint involved.

Follow the directions for your particular brand of stripper. Shake the can thoroughly, then pour a small amount of stripper into a large, wide-mouthed container such as a coffee can. Brush the stripper on the wood surface in as thick a coat as possible. Brush in one direction only; don't "scrub" the stripper in.

Bubbles

The coated surface should begin to bubble in a few moments as the old finish loosens. If areas appear to stay dry or don't bubble, recoat them with stripper and wait a bit longer. The entire surface should bubble up. This may take no more than a couple of minutes, or it may take as long as fifteen to twenty minutes, depending on the type of stripper and the type of finish being removed. Make a test scrape with your scraper to determine whether the finish has been thoroughly loosened. If the finish hasn't been loosened enough, apply more stripper. Don't attempt to remove stripper already in place. If the stripper begins to dry out, apply another layer. Keep the wood surface wet with stripper until it has enough time to dissolve the finish.

Several layers of different finish can be a problem, particularly where a layer of latex paint is over a layer of oil paint. The stripper

Allow remover plenty of time to work. Entire surface should bubble. Apply more remover to prevent surface from drying before it bubbles.

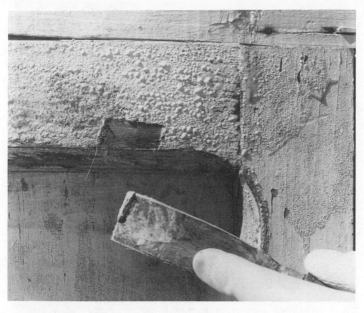

Make a test scrape of the surface.

If some finish remains after test scrape, add extra coats of remover.

When surface is loosened, scrape away finish and remover with a scraper or putty knife.

may cut through only the top layer of paint. You may have to remove the bulk of the stripper and the layer with a scraper, then start anew with the next layer of paint.

Use Large Scraper

Once you have determined by test scraping that the finish has been thoroughly loosened, use the largest scraper you can find to remove the bulk of the material from the wide flat surfaces of the wood. To prevent a mess, this material can be scraped off and placed in an old can or newspapers to be discarded. If the finish has been loosened properly it will skim away easily with a light pass of a scraper or putty knife. You shouldn't have to scrape or cut the material away. Use medium and coarse steel wool to remove the bulk of the material from turnings and carvings. If you are using a water-soluble remover take the piece outside and hose off the rest of the remover and old finish. Use a medium steel wool dipped in clean water to get the bits and pieces out of the cracks and crevices.

After scraping, hose away the remainder. Caution: the remover will kill grass.

If the remover is not water-soluble make sure you get off all remover and finish, then clean the surface with cleaner recommended by the manufacturer of the stripper. One of the best cleaning methods is to dip pieces of fine steel wool in clean water to which a bit of trisodium phosphate or a heavy-duty detergent containing TSP has been added. Use this to scrub away all the stains left by the drying remover. To get a smooth stripping job, keep the entire surface wet with either stripper or water until all finish and remover have been removed.

A stain with a permanganate base was used on much of the older furniture. If you are trying to remove such a stain, remove the finish, allow the project to dry thoroughly, then apply another coat of stripper to pull the stain out of the wood surface. If the stain doesn't disappear, try bleaching the surface by washing it with a mild solution of household bleach and water, then rinsing well with clean water.

Surface Preparation

When the finish has been removed, place the project in a cool, dry place. When it is dry, you should clean it thoroughly. In most cases the grain of the surface will be raised just a bit, and the surface should be sanded or steel-wooled to smooth it.

How smooth to make the surface is a personal choice, and also depends on what type of furniture is being refinished. In most cases, and particularly with primitive and antique furniture, it is best to under-sand than over-sand. This will leave a "patina," a light tan color, rather than the light color of freshly sanded or planed wood. Sanding may destroy some of the character left by scratches, mars, and worn corners.

All tiny bits of finish or paint, however, must be removed. Even with the best stripping job there will be flecks of loosened finish and remover down in the cracks. Those often can be removed with a small scraper, or a piece of medium steel wool. Even if you wish to do very little smoothing you should use fine steel wool to cut down the raised grain of the wood and make the entire wood surface as smooth as possible.

Always sand *with* the grain. Otherwise you will leave cross-grain

Sometimes you may want to sand finely to remove raised grain. Remember this may destroy the patina.

Clean the finish of all sanding dust and bits of loosened finish. A shop vacuum helps.

marks that are extremely hard to remove and will stick out like a sore thumb once the new finish or stain is applied. If you must use a coarse sandpaper in some areas, use progressively finer grits of sandpaper, then finish with steel wool to take out the marks left by the sandpapers. Rub the entire project with an old cotton glove or soft cloth to detect any rough spots or raised grain.

Remove Dust

After the surface has been smoothed correctly, all sanding dust and debris must be removed. A good shop vacuum will help pull dust out of cracks and crevices.

Wash down the wood surface with a bit of lacquer thinner and a soft cloth. If you have left the stripped project for a month or so, wash it down again with lacquer thinner to remove any dirt or oil before resuming work on it. Allow the surface to dry thoroughly, then use a tack cloth to remove all dirt, debris, and oily fingerprints. These cloths are available at most paint and hardware stores. Have several on hand. In an emergency you can make your own tack cloth by sprinkling a bit of varnish on a clean piece of linen or cheesecloth, and working the varnish into the cloth until it is well saturated. When using the tack cloth, keep turning it so you have a clean surface. Don't scrub with it; use it as a magnet to pick up dust and dirt from the surface.

Staining

It's a good idea to test the stain before starting a project. Pick an inconspicuous spot, such as the back of a chest or the bottom of a chair; you'll learn how the wood will take the stain, and whether the shade is the one you want.

You may not wish to stain a quality antique pine piece of furniture. If the piece is stripped properly and prepared without damaging the patina, a finish applied directly to the surface after cleaning will result in the mellow pumpkin pie color and appearance that is traditional with many early American styles of furniture.

Selecting the Stain

You may wish, however, to stain the piece to match other furniture in your home, or to bring out the grain of the wood. Picking the right stain and color is by far the hardest part of staining. There are hundreds of colors and types of stains on the market, even stains that are red, blue, green, and yellow, plus all the traditional wood grain stains. There are many types of special formulated stains, but for the average do-it-yourself refinisher there are basically three types of stains: penetrating oil, non-penetrating oil, and water-based.

Penetrating Oil Stains

These oil-based stains penetrate the pores of the wood to create a deep, yet very transparent stain. These are difficult for the beginner to use because they dry so quickly. It is hard to prevent lap marks and streaks where the stain is applied in an overlapped pattern, or where differences in the grain of the wood produce a hard and a

Brush on a penetrating-oil stain or a water-based stain. Make sure all excess is brushed away, and no runs or streaks are created.

soft spot that absorb the stain differently. Wipe them on with a clean cloth, quickly wiping away excess or adding more to fill in a light spot. All of a single surface must be stained at the same time.

Many of the newer penetrating stains are called controlled penetration, which means they will penetrate very slowly, and these are quite a bit easier to use. If applied correctly, penetrating oil stain is one of the most attractive for pine furniture.

A non-penetrating oil stain is first brushed on.

Non-Penetrating Oil Stain

A non-penetrating oil stain is by far the easiest stain for the average refinisher to use. It is known as a wiping stain because it is placed on the surface in a full flowing coat with a soft bristle brush. The stain is fairly opaque. Allow it to dry to a dull appearance, then wipe off the excess with a soft cloth dipped in stain and wrung out. By wiping away more in one area than another you can control the color and make light and dark streaks in the wood surface to match uneven grain patterns. Different colors can be mixed together to achieve almost any color. Because it dries slowly and doesn't penetrate the surface as does penetrating oil, you can work much more slowly. If you make a mistake, wipe it away and start over.

Allow non-penetrating oil stain to dry until a bit tacky, then wipe away surplus with a soft lint-free cloth.

The lengthy drying time for non-penetrating oil can cause two problems. One is the amount of lint that the stain picks up as it dries. Runs and streaks also can start on a vertical area long after you have wiped down the surface and left it to dry. Keep an eye out for this.

Non-penetrating oil is a good stain for pine because it normally results in a more even-toned finish. With hard-grained pines it may be wiped away too easily especially if you want a dark, fairly opaque finish such as is popular today with country English-style pine furniture.

Sometimes a filler is applied with the stain or just after. This isn't necessary when refinishing pine furniture because the pores are so tight and smooth.

Water-Based Stains

Water-based stains, the favorites of professionals, give a brilliant and pleasing appearance to pine furniture. They consist of aniline dyes that are mixed with water to provide the tone and depth of stain. They are brushed on in smooth, even coats. While quite inexpensive, they may be difficult to find, and you may have to order them from specialty shops. They are the most transparent of stains and will help to give a patina to an old piece of furniture that has been over-sanded or over-stripped.

Finishing

Once the stain has dried thoroughly you're ready for the finishing process. Many people think applying a good finish on a piece of furniture is a magical act that only the pros can accomplish. It's far from that; the average do-it-yourselfer can apply a much better finish than can the professionals because he spends more time on the project. That's what a good finish requires — time, careful attention to cleanliness, and patience.

Find a well-lit, clean, dust-free room or area for this process. It can be nothing more than the kitchen table for small projects, if plenty of newspapers are used to cover the table.

For larger projects you may wish to vacuum your garage, and use it as a work area. Have on hand plenty of newspapers to catch drips, soft cloths for applying finish or for cleaning, and the appropriate thinner to remove finish from hands and brushes.

If a can of finish has been opened earlier, it's a good idea to strain the finish through a discarded nylon stocking to remove dust or bits of dry finish.

Stir, Don't Shake

Most clear finishes don't require shaking; however, a bit of gentle stirring may be needed. Shaking often produces air bubbles that dry in the finish. This is a real problem with heavy varnishes that dry slowly. Read the label on the can for specific instructions.

If using brushes for applying the finish, make sure they're good quality and clean. They should have nylon or natural bristles. If the finish is to be applied with a cloth use only soft, lint-free material such as an old T-shirt.

A great number of finishes are available to the refinisher. Five finishes are good with pine furniture: combination shellac-and-paste wax, penetrating resin, rubbed oil finish, varnish, and lacquer. Each has its advantages and disadvantages. Use only quality name-brand finishes, and don't mix different kinds or even different brands together to save on materials.

Varnish

The most commonly applied finish is a varnish. There are gloss varnishes and satin finish or eggshell varnishes. The choice is a matter of personal preference; however, most pine furniture looks best with a minimum of gloss and shine. Varnish is the easiest of finishes to apply, yet one of the hardest to apply correctly. Because it dries slowly, it will pick up lint and dust from the air. A great deal of effort must be spent on cleanliness.

Probably the most popular type of varnish today is the polyurethane wood finish, an extremely hard, durable finish that is excellent for bar tops and floors. A natural varnish such as tung varnish isn't quite as hard, yet is fine for furniture because it doesn't become brittle with age. It dries more slowly than polyurethane varnish.

Seal First

Any wood that is to be finished with varnish must first be sealed. This is usually done with a thin coat of shellac, however varnish can be thinned to about half strength and applied as a sealer. Varnish should never be applied directly over a non-penetrating oil stain because the pigment of the stain lies on the surface and is dissolved by the varnish, causing a cloudy, streaked effect. Make sure there are no oily fingerprints on the surface or the varnish won't "stick" in that particular area.

Varnish should be applied in a warm, dry place. In cold weather use a heat lamp or small heater to warm the project before applying the finish and then to hasten drying. At room temperatures varnish will set in about eight hours, however it probably won't be completely dry for at least twenty-four hours. Thus, applying several coats takes quite a bit of time. For instance the glossy "piano" finish requires at least twenty-five coats of hand-rubbed varnish. One test for dryness of the varnish coat is to make a fingerprint on a surface that won't be seen, such as on the underside of a chair arm. Then try to wipe away the fingerprint. If it won't wipe away with a soft cloth the varnish hasn't cured.

One of the biggest problems with proper application of varnish is overloading the brush. Only the bottom fourth or third of the brush should be dipped in the varnish. This is then brought up against the edge of the can and most of the varnish dragged off, or as professionals say, "tipped off." You can make a varnish can for tipping by running a piece of stiff wire through the top of a can.

With the brush properly loaded with varnish, make a smooth clean stroke against the grain to apply the varnish. Make the second stroke overlapping the first. After all the surface has been coated in this manner, stroke with the grain, again overlapping the edges of the strokes. Each time you apply more varnish go from the dry surface into the wet to prevent leaving brush-starting marks in the previously applied varnish. Lift the brush gently with a sweeping motion. Varnish should never be scrubbed in; this only causes more bubbles. The more you work the surface the more bubbles you will have. Use light, smooth sweeping strokes and don't apply too much varnish at one coat. It takes several coats for a good, smooth finish.

Varnish only a small area at a time, and if possible keep the surface horizontal to prevent sags and runs. These can be picked up with a brush that has been dipped in varnish, then almost all finish tipped off.

Lint or bubbles can be removed by using an artist's brush to which a bit of varnish has been applied and allowed to become tacky. Again, however, don't overwork the surface, as many of the

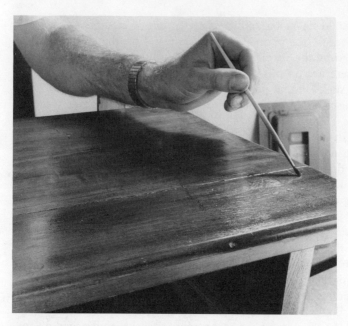

Small bits of lint, dirt or bubbles can be removed from a varnish finish with a small paint brush which has a bit of tacky varnish on it.

finer bubbles will be removed when the finish is sanded. Allow to dry thoroughly. After at least a couple days' drying time, sand the surface of the varnish with 6/0 garnet paper, then remove all sanding dust, wipe the surface with a tack cloth, and apply the second coat. After the second coat has dried thoroughly, sand with 6/0 wet-or-dry sandpaper, and use a bit of Ivory soap and water as a protective sludge. Succeeding coats are smoothed down with extra fine steel wool. After you have applied each finish, leave the room and close the door. Foot traffic can create a lot of dust problems.

After the final varnish coat, a coat of wax and polish is applied as will be discussed later.

Rubbed Oil Finish

Probably the oldest finish in America is the rubbed oil finish. In the pioneer days warm linseed oil was rubbed into a wood surface.

The hand-rubbed oil finish. Craftsmen used to heat the varnish and turpentine in a double boiler, then apply it with a soft cloth and buff.

The palm of the hand was used to rub and polish the wood surface to a soft, smooth finish. This type of finish is one of the most economical, but it takes a great deal of time and elbow grease. It looks great with many early American pieces of pine furniture. Try this finish on a small project first, to see whether you have the patience to do it.

To make up the finish, mix together three parts boiled linseed oil with one part turpentine, and warm in a double boiler. Remember both of these are flammable chemicals. Don't let the mixture boil over.

To apply, flow the solution onto the surface in a full thick coat and allow it to soak in for twenty to thirty minutes. With a soft cloth wipe away the surplus and buff the remainder into the wood using steel wool. It usually will take about twenty to twenty-five coats of finish to acquire the deep, hand-polished look. The last coat can be polished with extra fine steel wool, then with the palm of your hand.

There are many substitute oil hand-rubbed finishes today that give the same appearance, yet are quite a bit easier to apply, such as those by Minwax and the Birchwood Casey Company.

Penetrating Oil Finishes

These penetrating resin finishes are quite similar to the old hand-rubbed oil finishes except they aren't rubbed off in the same manner. They are fine for more modern pieces of pine furniture. With these finishes you don't sand between coats, so the surface penetration has to be extra good.

If possible, the surface should be horizontal. Flood the surface with the penetrating resin and keep the entire surface wet with the solution for about an hour. Then wipe off excess finish with soft lint-free cloth and polish with a bit of paste wax and steel wool. All excess finish must be removed within one hour, or before it starts to become tacky.

Lacquer

Lacquer is a relatively modern finish produced from nitrocellulose and with an acetone-based solvent. It can't be applied over varnishes or enamels as it will bubble up. All old finish must be removed thoroughly before the lacquer is applied.

There are two basic styles of lacquer; high gloss, which is often used on bar tops and piano cases, and an eggshell or satin finish, which is most often used for furniture.

Lacquer is the finish preferred by many professional refinishers, mainly because of the ease in application and because it dries quickly. A coat of lacquer, if applied properly, will dry within five to twenty minutes, and then can be smoothed down and a second coat applied. Although there are many types of lacquer including opaque automotive and metal work finishes, those used for wood refinishing are clear brushing and spraying lacquers. About the only difference between the two is that the brushing lacquer dries more slowly, giving you time for proper application.

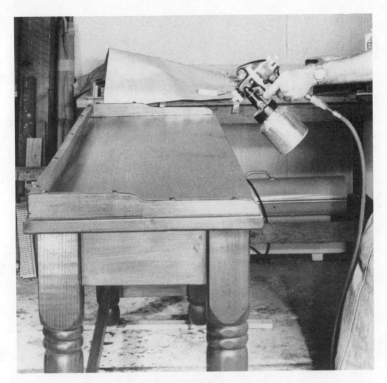

The sprayed lacquer finish is fastest to apply, and easiest, once the process is learned.

Flow It On

Brushing lacquer is fairly easy to use, however it must be flowed on quickly with a large clean brush, rather than worked into the surface. Avoid lap marks as much as possible and keep from brushing off the surface. Brushing lacquer is available in both gloss and satin finishes.

The majority of lacquer finishes are sprayed on with spray gun equipment. When properly applied, sprayed lacquer is sturdy and one of the most transparent finishes. It is resistant to water, alcohol, and abuse. It produces a finish with the least amount of color change in the wood.

Clean Surface

To get a good lacquer finish, the wood surface must be as smooth and clean as possible. The first coat should be a sealer coat of half lacquer and half thinner, or better yet a coat of sanding-sealer lacquer. After the sealer has dried, cut off the raised grain with extremely fine finishing sandpaper (extremely fine steel wool may be used for rounded surfaces). Then wipe off the surface with a tack cloth. The finish will be chalky white and may look ruined, but with the next coat it will clear up entirely. It takes several coats of lacquer to make a good finish. Sand or steel-wool between coats to cut down the wood fibers that are raised.

A good external mix spray gun coupled with a compressor that will produce at least forty-five pounds of pressure is necessary in

A compressor is needed for spraying lacquer.

order to spray lacquer properly. Thin the lacquer with lacquer thinner only according to the manufacturer's instructions. This may be as much as 35 to 50 percent.

Explosive — Watch Out

Lacquer and lacquer thinner are highly explosive. Spray outside, away from all flames. If spraying inside a building, make sure all open flames, including pilot lights and water heaters, are extinguished. Provide plenty of ventilation, including a fan if necessary to exhaust the fumes.

After thinning the lacquer according to manufacturer's instructions, test spray a bit of waste wood so you can determine whether the gun is working properly and the proper spray is being achieved. You should have a good even spray pattern when the gun is held from six to ten inches away from the wood surface.

Spray all corners and rounded surfaces first, making sure you keep the gun moving so you don't create runs or sag. A run or sag on a lacquer finish is a real problem as it dries so quickly you can't wipe it away, and even then the wiped area will show with the final finish. This is a case where prevention is essential. Make sure you apply the spray in thin even coats and that the gun cup doesn't drip lacquer onto the surface beneath it.

Keep Gun Parallel to Surface

The one most common mistake most beginners make when spraying finishes is to move the gun in an arc. Instead, keep the gun parallel to the wood surface at all times. Also make sure you are outside the edges of a surface before starting the gun, otherwise you will create an unevenly sprayed surface. Spray first across the grain, then with the grain for the first coat. All additional coats should be with the grain. Move the gun slowly but steadily. If you hold the gun too close it will create runs. If the gun is too far away it will cause "orange peel" or a roughened surface. If the gun is using too much air this same situation will be created. If you get pinholes in the surface the lacquer is too thick. If there is an opaque "blushing" or "film" the weather is too humid.

After the final coat, apply a coat of paste wax and buff, as will be discussed later.

Several coats of water-resistant, alcohol-resistant satin-finish lacquer followed by the proper amount of buffing and polishing is my favorite finish. Because we have three children, all my furniture is finished so it can take the wear and abuse.

Although many aerosol cans may list their contents as lacquer, they're usually acrylic and not suitable for a good lacquer finish on wood.

After using the spray gun, clean it thoroughly by pouring out any mixed lacquer (keep this in a clean jar for future use), and fill the gun cup with lacquer thinner. Spray a bit of the thinner through the gun. If you won't be using the gun for some time you may wish to remove the nozzle and soak it in lacquer thinner. Wipe off any spilled lacquer on the cup, especially around the threads on the top. A buildup of lacquer can prevent the cup and gun top from sealing properly. The resulting leaks can cause lacquer drips on a finished surface.

Shellac and Wax

This is one of the oldest and probably the easiest finish to apply to pine furniture. The wood surface must be absolutely smooth. The first coat is a very thin coat of shellac thinned with alcohol. This acts as a sealer. Work with the grain and quickly because the material dries quite fast, but avoid brushing it out too much. After a sealer coat apply additional coats of shellac thinned according to the manufacturer's instructions. Sand between each coat with fine sandpaper or steel wool. After the last coat use pumice stone and water to smooth down. Follow that with a coat of paste wax well buffed with steel wool.

Finish Amalgamators

If you have a piece of pine furniture with a relatively good finish, except that the finish is dried out, cracked, or dirty, consider using one of the amalgamating finishes. These have a solvent base that

If the old finish is satisfactory, use an amalgamator to clean it.

partially dissolves some older softer finishes, allowing them to be cleaned up and rubbed in a bit more at the same time. One of the more popular brands is Formsby's Refinisher. These are rubbed on-to and into the finish to blend and smooth it together. At the same time it usually cleans off dirt and grime that have built up on the finish.

Polishing

Once the final coat of finish has been applied, regardless of whether it is varnish or lacquer, you can improve on the final appearance by rubbing and polishing with the proper materials. This job well done is the mark of a caring craftsperson. Quite often a lot of work is spent in stripping, staining, and finishing a project, but then it is left. A little more work would produce a much smoother and more professional finish.

Regardless of how careful you are in applying a finish there will be some imperfections including dull and shiny spots, or an unevenly applied finish, or dust or bubbles in the finish. In some cases the finish may be too glossy and you may wish to dull it down a bit.

In most cases if the finish has been applied properly you will need to do nothing more than apply a bit of paste floor wax with a soft cloth, then buff with steel wool. Follow this with an application of a good quality furniture polish.

On the other hand, some finishes may require more work. You should start off with a bit of pumice stone sprinkled on the surface.

For a fine finish, polish with pumice stone and a bit of water to create a slurry, and use felt on a wooden block.

Wet this with either water or rubbing oil (available at most paint stores). This abrasive paste should be rubbed over the surface using a piece of felt wrapped around a small piece of wood.

Watch the surface carefully and rub until the entire surface is clean and smooth and even appearing. Be careful not to rub through the surface on corners and rounded areas. A tiny piece of felt can be used for these places. In most cases this will produce a satin surface. If you wish to increase the shine repeat this step, using rottenstone as the abrasive powder. Rottenstone powder is so fine that it takes quite a bit of elbow grease to get the finish polished down smoothly and with a nice even gloss.

Follow this step with rottenstone powder.

Clean, then apply paste floor wax.

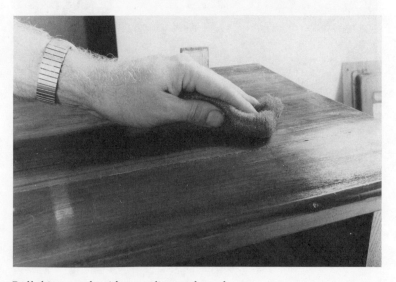

Buff this smooth with extra fine steel wool.

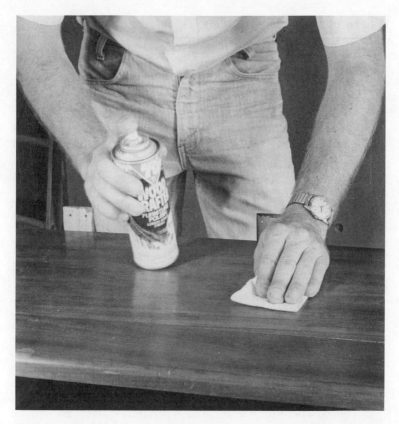

And finish with a coat of furniture polish.

The final steps, shown in the three photographs on these pages, are simple ones. Clean the surface of your furniture thoroughly, apply a thin layer of paste floor wax, rub this in, then buff it smooth with the extra-fine steel wool. Finally, rub in a coat of furniture polish.

Now call in your friends. You've completed a project they should admire with you.

Where to Purchase Supplies

Birchwood Casey Co.
7900 Fuller Rd.
Eden Prairie, MN 55343

Constantine's
2050 Eastchester Rd.
The Bronx, NY 10461

Craftsman Wood Service
2727 S. Mary St.
Addison, IL 60101

Minwax Co., Inc.
175 West Cortland Court
Addison, IL 60101